# A Soldier's Wife Cookbook

W0006598

## Written By
## Linda Marie Thomas

PublishAmerica
Baltimore

ISBN: 1-60474-325-5
PUBLISHED BY PUBLISHAMERICA, LLLP
www.publishamerica.com
Baltimore

Printed in the United States of America

# DEDICATIONS AND ACKNOWLEDGMENTS

I would like to thank every one of you who have shown support for the troops and there families. We as military families truly appreciate it whenever we see a support our troops sign on a car or truck, a banner on a business building, an American Flag blowing in the wind, or a yellow ribbon tied around a tree in a yard. Your sincere concerns and support help the military families with emotional support during any deployment. Being a military wife and mother of a soldier, I take great pride in both my husband and my son. By becoming a Soldiers wife I have come to live a very unique lifestyle. Sometimes pressure becomes so great that my life as a military wife is affected tremendously, but if you were to ask any military wife how they cope, they would tell you proudly that it is there faith in god and love and support from the military unit, family, friends and other caring civilians like you who are willing to put forth that extra effort to show our troops just how much you care.

Thanks to SFC. Adrian S. Thomas, my loving husband for always telling me to never give up on any of my dreams, this book is dedicated to you Soldier. I love you for always supporting me and for loving me unconditionally. I could have never done this without you.

Thank you Christopher, Carlos, Adrian, Ara, and Krishonsti for all of your love and support and encouragement over the years, I love all of you with all of my heart, and always remember that the best is yet to come.

Thanks to Verna and Cleveland Eggins for you are the best parents in the world and my first cooking teachers, I love the both of you so very much.

Thanks to my siblings Evelyn Alston, Charlene Suttice, and Terry Eggins I love you with all of my heart, and all of my nieces and nephew.

Thanks to my grandmother Rosa Howard for allowing me to help her in the kitchen and for teaching me how to cook at such an early age.

Thanks to Ruth and Bobby Racheal you are the best Aunt and Uncle in the world, and I love you.

Thanks to: Drayton and Thomas Family, Lucy Chavez, Mrs. Montgomery, and the students and staff at Clear Creek Elementary in Fort Hood Texas, and to Dee Bulliner and family, Judy McGill, Marcie Speight, Mary M., and Cindy M. and Mr. Wilbur at Purvis Post Office I love you guys.

Special Thanks to all of the doctors, nurses, and staff at Darnell Community Hospital in Fort Hood Texas, and to Dr. Diamond, Dr. Washburne, Dr. Azar and staff in Hattiesburg Mississippi you guys are the best.

Special Thanks to Oprah Winfrey for always recognizing and thanking teachers, and stay at home mothers for having the hardest job there is. You have inspired me to live my best life and I thank you from the heart. I appreciate you and all that you do for others.

You are truly blessed, and to me you are indeed one of Gods Angels.

# How I Met and Married My Soldier

My book is entitled A Soldiers Wife Cook Book this cookbook is a
dream come true for me because I have always wanted to write a
cook book and in it tell a short story about how I met and married my
soldier. I also wanted to share many of my Soldiers favorite recipes.
I hope that you enjoy the story and all of the wonderful recipes in the
book. I met my Soldier SFC. Adrian S. Thomas in 1985 when he was
stationed at Fort Polk Army Base located in Leesville Louisiana.

I was a single mother of two young boys. I had been married
once before but that marriage ended in a divorce.

I dated for a while after the divorce and decided to give dating up
to, due to the fact that I felt that I needed to go through a healing
process before allowing myself to get involved in another relationship.
I decided to put all of my focus and energy on my two boys, who at
the time were very young and growing very fast.

My boys and I have always had wonderful times together I was
playing the role of both mother and father to them. It was not easy
but it was what I felt that I had to do. I wanted my boys to have a
great life, and they did. Thanks to my loving parents Cleveland and
Verna Eggins who helped me out a lot.

Let me began my story by telling you about the very first time I
saw Adrian S. Thomas my soldier. It was a summer day in June of
1985 that I decided to go to the beach with a girl friend of mine.

She and I went to the beach on a Sunday afternoon to talk and
relax, while there we saw a group of fine young soldiers who were

just sitting around under a palm tree laughing and talking. As we walked past the soldiers we said hello trying not to make eye contact with any of them. They were all very attractive, from what I saw with a quick glance. We giggled like young school girls making comments to each other on how handsome the soldiers were. I was not at all interested in becoming seriously involved in a relationship with anyone. I had made up my mind that all I wanted was to concentrate on my life as a young single divorced mother of two young boys and how to best raise them to become respectable young men.

The following weekend I was invited to go out with my best friend Catherine, my sister Evelyn and her then fiancé, now husband Andre, who at the time was also a soldier. I accepted the invitation.

On that night I was having a great time laughing and talking with them, and while we were sitting at the table having great conversation a group of soldiers walked in and walked up to the table where we were sitting and they began to talk to Andre Alston.

In the group of soldiers there was this one soldier that caught my eye, I thought that he was cute he was tall so he stood out in the crowd. It was, Adrian.

He and I made eye contact and he came and stood by where I was sitting and asked me what my name was.

I told him and we began to talk. He asked me to dance with him but I told him no. I wanted to say yes but no came out of my mouth instead. I knew when I saw him that there was something about him that seemed familiar, but I did not know exactly what it was, except for the fact that he was a very handsome man.

I did not believe in love at first site but wondered what could it be?

I did not know what exactly peeked my curiosity so strongly in this man.

Earlier during the day I had a talk with the Lord. I told the Lord that I was happy with my life and that I was not looking for any man to be in my life at this particular time that I was content.

But if I would meet someone that was worth my time, I would

like for him to be a preacher's son and I wanted him to be honest, loving, and kind and great with children and someone whom I could trust with my heart. I thanked God for my boys and asked Him to bless the three of us. I would always have conversations with the Lord. But I do not know until this very day why I asked the Lord to send a preacher's son into my life, but I did. I often laugh when I think about my conversation that I had with the Lord that day. But to be honest I was truly sincere.

Later that night I met Adrian, the first words that came out of his mouth were, and "I have seen you before". I laughed at him and said to myself he is such a liar and this is just another sorry pick up line.

He went on to say that he was a preacher's grandson, when he said that he had my attention because at that very moment a light went off in my head and I remembered my conversation that I had had with the Lord earlier that day. He was not a preacher's son but a grandson, I kept repeating in my head, close enough I said to myself jokingly.

Adrian went on to tell me how his grandfather had helped to raise him and how his grandfather was like a father to him. I thought about my sons and how my father was taking the roll of father figure in there lives and I began to ask questions.

I asked him did it bother him that his father was not a part of his life and he said "To be honest yes, but went on to say that he was grateful for the role that his grandfather played in his life. He learned a lot from him and appreciated him for it was his grandfather that taught him how to be a good man. All men are not meant to be fathers but for those who are and take their role of being a father seriously I commend them. I did not want to bring a cloud over the conversation or make it depressing so I apologized for asking so many personal questions. He told me that it was okay. He then smiled at me and began to tell me where he had first seen me.

I was shocked because he was not lying nor was he giving me a pick up line, he truly had seen me before; It was the day that I had went walking on the beach with my friend. He remembered me.

He was one of those very attractive soldiers that my girlfriend and I had seen on the beach that Sunday.

Adrian and I had talked for hours and hours it seemed. When I left that night I thought to myself that he was an interesting man, and it would be wonderful if he could possibly be the man that I had talked to the lord about. I wanted to see him again but I did not know how I was to go about it. Remember I was not looking for a man to be in my life. I was not a bold woman so walking up to any man and telling him that I was interested in him to me was being to forward and I was not going to do anything like that no matter how much I wanted to see him again.

I reminded myself that all I wanted was a life without drama, because I had been married before and that relationship left me somewhat bitter, it was not a good one for me. I was not the kind of woman that felt that she had to have a man in her life to be happy or complete. But after meeting Adrian I was willing to give the right man a chance if and when I met him, I had no idea that Adrian would be that man.

Adrian and I had not exchanged phone numbers, and he left early that night with his friends, but on the ride home with my sister and her fiancé, all I talked about was Adrian. I asked Andre to tell me everything that he knew about him. Andre filled me in on everything that he knew and he told me that he was single, and that he and Adrian had served in Germany together, he went on to say that he thought that he was a good guy and that Adrian would spend his spare time lifting weights. That was not a lot but it was all good things nothing bad.

The next day I told my mother about Adrian, she listened to me as I rambled on an on about how we talked all night, I acted like I did not like him. My mother laughed at me and told me that this man that I had met was going to be my husband in two years. I looked at my mother and said that I would never get married again.

She said I know what you said darling, but I am telling you what is going to happen. My mother told me to go and get a calendar and I did and on the calendar she circled a month. She looked at me and told me that I would be married within a year or two to Adrian. I took the calendar out of her hand to see what she had circled on it she had circled the month of June. I asked my mother how she could be so sure, because this was a man that I had just met. My mother knew how I felt about marriage; after my first marriage ended the way that it did I had issues with trust, because my first husband cheated.

Mother told me that she could not explain it but she knew that Adrian would be my husband. My sisters and I laughed at mother but we knew from years of living with her that whenever she would say something it always happened the way that she said that it would. It was the strangest thing but her words of wisdom never failed to come true.

I could not even imagine being married to anyone, especially this soldier that I had just met. Marriage was the farthest thing from my mind.

I saw Adrian again the following weekend and we talked and talked again for hours. We lost ourselves in conversation. We had so many things in common, his birthday was October 8, 1965 and my birthday was October 15, 1960. His mother's birthday was on October fifteenth, and his father's birthday was on a day after mine. We also enjoyed so many of the same things.

Adrian loved poetry, art, and antiques, watching old movies and fishing only to name a few things, and so did I.

It was only after we decided to date each other that I introduced him to the loves of my life and that was my two sons, Christopher and Carlos. When the boys met Adrian they thought that he was the best. Months had past and he would visit every weekend. That he could. Adrian became my best friend.

Adrian is very romantic and he never forgets a birthday or anniversary and he always put great thought into any cards or gifts that he gives.

After two years of dating him he asked me to marry him. The first time that Adrian asked me to marry him I said No!

Not because I didn't love him, I said No because I was afraid. I had a fear of getting married again and then having it end in divorce.

I told him how I felt and he told me that if I would accept his hand in marriage that it would be forever. I looked into his eyes and said,

9

"Forever is a long time and I hope, that this promise can be kept." I was so afraid but so in love with him.

He took my hand and placed the ring on my finger and asked me to marry him again and this time I said yes. Something inside let me know that it was right.

We got married on June 20, 1987. It was a very beautiful day one that I will remember for the rest of my life. Reverend Fobbs performed the wedding ceremony. My sisters, Evelyn and Charlene were in the wedding and the church was filled with family and friends. On June 20, 1987 I felt like a princess, everything was beautiful to me that day. After the wedding ceremony, we went to our reception, while sitting in the limousine Adrian turned to me and told me that he was the happiest man in the world and that he was going to be the best husband and father to me and my boys. I knew at that very moment that life with him and the boys was going to be a great one, and it truly has been.

We have four children now and one grandchild. Christopher age 29, Carlos age 22 Adrian age 19, Ara age 16 and my one and only grandchild Khrishonsti age 7. She is the daughter of my oldest son.

Adrian is truly a family man and he has always made family a top priority. Being a soldier's wife is an exciting, adventurous and sometimes stressful life especially when your soldier has to be deployed to war or another country without the family.

You miss them and you think of them the entire time that they are gone. But you learn to cope with the fact that this is his job, and you learn to keep your family together the best way that you can. You attend support group meetings and become very creative with doing activities with your children to make the deployment less stressful on them and yourself.

I would not trade being a Soldier's wife for anything.

I am proud of my husband and I love him with all of my heart.

He not only completes me, but he compliments my life. I could not imagine living without him and our children because they are the love that keeps my heart beating.

Cooking is something that I have always enjoyed doing with my children and my mother and grandmother were my first and very best teachers. I enjoy preparing food for my Soldier, and he enjoys eating, Adrian is a very good cook himself, and he and the children have prepared me some wonderful meals. But those meals only come on special occasions like anniversaries, birthdays, Christmas morning, and on those days when I might be feeling a little under the weather.

My Soldier is an amazing man whom I am very proud of and love with all of my heart. I believe that there is a great strength in a Soldier, and after Hurricane Katrina hit the house that we lived in causing enormous damage, I witness my Soldiers strength as we sit inside of a house and the trees all around us falling trapping us inside. Doors being blown open even though they were supposed to be locked. Water pouring into the house like a waterfall I watched him get hit by a huge tree that came crashing through the roof of our house and knocked him to the floor, my daughter called 911 for help but they were unable to get to us because of all of the fallen trees and deprive in the roads, and when they finally got to the house where we lived and cut there way through all of the fallen trees my husband would not leave us, instead of him leaving with the paramedics to seek care for himself he remained at the house with me and the children only to make sure that would be safe, and I must say that after seeing with my own eyes my soldier come so close to death, I am even more amazed by his strength and courage. I thank the Lord for allowing my family to survive the storm, and for wrapping his loving arms around my husband on that day. If my husband would not have fallen to the floor when he did, the Long Branch from another tree that came crashing through the roof would have gone straight through his chest. We are truly blessed, and grateful to the Lord for saving him.

I would like to share with you my soldiers favorite poem entitled THE OLD CATHEDRAL written by, Linda Eggins Thomas.

11

## The Old Cathedral

The old cathedral's roof is leaking but it still manages to stand.
The doors are almost off of their hinges.
Some of the windows are broken.
There is still this beautiful look about it that welcomes you to
walk inside
Once you have entered you feel your soul began to emerge,
because this is where it wants to abide.
A glorious sound of Amazing Grace suddenly comes to mind
You close your eyes and say a prayer
So overwhelmed by the experience you began to cry.
Brilliant gleams of light shine through the stain glass windows
Vines grow wildly all over the trellis that once had them trained.
Wild flowers bloom in a multitude of colors
Weeds smother the lawn that once was a beautiful shade of
green
Close your eyes for only a moment, and imagine hearing Angels
sing.
Birds sit in the treetops until early dawn
Bee's dance around the morning glory
The cathedral is old and forgotten but it still holds a sacred
story.

# BEVERAGES

# BANANA PUNCH

3 cups water

2 ½ cup sugar

1 can (46 oz.) pineapple juice

2 ½ orange juice

4 ripe bananas mashed

3 qt. ginger ale chilled

Mix water and sugar in saucepan and bring to a boil.
Remove from heat and stir in the fruit juices and mashed bananas
Pour into trays or cartons and freeze until firm to serve; Remove
And let stand 10-15 minutes to soften fruit mixture.
Break mixture into chunks. Pour ginger ale over it then serve.
Makes about 24 servings in tall glasses

# BRANDY PUNCH

1 fifth brandy

4 qt. iced tea

1 ½ cup sugar

1 frozen molded ring of ice

Pour brandy, tea, sugar and lemon juice over ice ring in punch bowl.
Stir until well blended. Frozen strawberries may be added to float on top.

# CHERRY PUNCH

1 can (6 ounces) frozen lemonade concentrate thawed

5 cups cherry juice chilled

1 bottle (28 ounces) water, chilled

Lemon slices for garnish mint sprigs for garnish

Reconstitute lemonade according to label directions in large punch bowl.
Add all remaining ingredients chill then serve.

# *EGG NOG*

1 dozen eggs

1 quart cream

1 ½ cup sugar

1 pint whiskey (only if you want alcohol)

Separate eggs. Beat yolks and add sugar until creamy.
Add whiskey slowly. Add whipped cream and stir well.
Whip half of the whites and add to the above mixture by folding them.
Chill well.

# EGG NOG

12 large eggs, lightly beaten

1 AND ½ cups sugar

4 cups half and half

4 cups milk

½ cup bourbon

¼ teaspoon salt

½ cup brandy

2 teaspoons vanilla

2 cups whipping cream

½ teaspoon ground nutmeg

Gradually you add sugar to eggs in a large glass bowl, whisk until blended. Then set aside.

Mix the half and half, milk, and salt in a Dutch oven over medium heat. Stirring occasionally for 15 minutes or until the mixture begins to bubble around the edge of the pan, do not boil.

Gradually stir half of the hot milk mixture into the egg mixture.

Stir egg mixture into hot milk mixture in the Dutch oven.

# FRUIT PUNCH

1 46-oz. can orange juice, or 2 cans frozen orange juice, reconstituted.
1 46-oz. cans pineapple juice
1qt. apple juice
1 qt. cranberry juice
1 16-oz. can frozen lemon juice
1 qt. water
¾ cup sugar
2 qt. ginger ale, chilled
2 oranges, thinly sliced and unpeeled

Mix all ingredients except ginger ale and orange slices, stirring to dissolve sugar. Chill overnight.
Pour over ice, add orange and ginger ale.
Serve and enjoy.

# FRUIT SHAKE

1 cup fresh or frozen strawberries
1 can of (6 ounces) pineapple juice chilled
1 medium banana peeled, Ice cubes

Then place all ingredients in blender process until smooth pour
Into a tall glass, garnish with a piece of fresh fruit or mint sprig.

# MIMI'S SMOOTHIE

½ cup of your favorite fruit juice

2 peeled bananas

1 cup frozen vanilla yogurt

1 cup of your favorite frozen fruits

Put all ingredients into the blender and process until smooth and then pour into glasses and add a straw and enjoy.

# RASPBERRY FRUIT JUICE PUNCH

2 cans frozen pineapple

2 cans frozen orange juice

3 cans frozen lemonade

2 cans frozen grapefruit juice

4 boxes frozen raspberries

Dilute all frozen juice according to instructions on cans and combine.
Crush frozen raspberries through food mill.
Freeze ½ of the amount of the raspberries to use in place of ice.
Mix remaining 2/3 of the raspberries with the above diluted juices.

# SPICED TEA

1 ½ cup instant tea with lemon

14 oz. jar instant orange breakfast drink mix

2 pkg. dry lemonade mix with sugar

2 tsp. ground cloves

2 tsp. cinnamon

Mix all of these dry ingredients together and store in a jar you need not refrigerate.

When ready to serve put 2 tsp. into a cup and fill the cup with hot water.

# STRAWBERRY PUNCH

1 ½ cup strawberries

1 ½ cup sugar

1 qt. ginger ale

3 cans frozen pink lemonade


Add sugar to strawberries. Make lemonade and chill.
Before serving add ginger ale and strawberries to lemonade.

# WHITE SANGRIA

2 cups fruity white wine

2 quarts of pineapple, orange and guava juice

¼ cup orange-flavored liqueur

¼ cup sugar

1 orange, thinly sliced

1 lime thinly sliced

2 cups sliced fresh strawberries

Ice cubes

Sprigs of mint for garnish

Combine all ingredients except ice and mint in a large pitcher, cover and refrigerate for 2 hours to blend flavors.
Serve over ice and garnish with mint sprigs or slice of orange.

# SALADS

# BLACK BEAN SALAD

2 cans black beans

1 jalapeno pepper

2 scallions

1 red onion

2 tomatoes

1 lime

1 teaspoon cilantro

In a bowl mix 2 cans of black beans drained and take a jalapeno pepper take out the seeds, and chop.

Dice the scallions, red onions, tomatoes squeeze in the lime juice then add cilantro toss together and serve.

# CAESAR SALAD

3 OR 4 cloves of garlic, diced

3 quarts Salad greens

½ cup parmesan cheese, grated

½ tsp. dry mustard

2 hard cooked eggs, chopped

1 cup olive oil

2 cup crisp croutons

½ cup unseasoned salad oil

¼ cup bleu cheese

# CHEF'S SALAD

1 large head lettuce

½ cup celery, sliced

½ cup green pepper, chopped

1 tomato cut in wedges

½ cucumber, sliced

½ cup French dressing

½ lb. cooked ham, salami, and chicken cut in strips.

¼ lb. longhorn cheese cut in strips

2 hard – cooked eggs, sliced

Break chilled lettuce into bowl, add other vegetables.
Toss well with dressing top with meat and cheese strips and cooked eggs

# CHICKEN SALAD

2 cups cooked chicken cubed

1 cup celery, chopped

2 tbsp. sweet pickles chopped

3 hard boiled eggs chopped

¼ cup crisp, bacon finely broken

2 tbsp. lemon juice

Salt and pepper

½ cup mayonnaise

Combine all ingredients; toss lightly. Chill thoroughly.

# CUCUMBER SALAD

2 large cucumbers

1 ¼ tsp. salt

1 cup sour cream

2 tbsp. lemon juice

1 tbsp. chopped onion

2 tbsp. chopped dill pickles

¼ tsp. sugar

Dash of pepper

3 radishes, thinly sliced

1 ½ tsp. parsley

Slice cucumbers about 1/8 inches thick.
You may leave the peeling on ½ of them to add color.
Slice radishes very thin and combine all ingredients.
Mix in a bowl and chill in refrigerator before serving.

# FRUIT SALAD

1 fresh pineapple

2 or 3 oranges, peeled and sliced

1 ½ cup strawberries

1 cup seedless green grapes

Strawberry- Banana Yogurt Dressing

1 ripe banana peeled

6 strawberries halved

1 carton 8 ounces vanilla yogurt

1 tablespoon brown sugar or honey

Cut pineapple in half lengthwise through crown
Cut fruit from shells with knife, leaving shells intact
Cut fruit into chunks. Combine pineapple, orange, bananas, strawberries and grape in large bowl, Spoon into pineapple shells.
Serve with strawberry- Banana yogurt

# GRILLED PINEAPPLE CHICKEN SALAD

1 ½ 8 ounces pineapple chunks in juice

1 tablespoon vegetables oil

1 tablespoon red wine vinegar

1 tablespoon chopped fresh dill or ½ teaspoon dried dill weed

1 large clove garlic, pressed

½ teaspoon sugar

½ teaspoon salt

Cracked black pepper to taste

2 boneless, skinless chicken breast halves

Salad greens

1 small red bell pepper cut into rings

1 grapefruit, peeled sliced, halved

2 tablespoons sliced green onion

Dill sprigs for garnish

Drain pineapple; reserve 1/3 cup juice.

For dressing, combine reserved juice, oil vinegar, dill, garlic, sugar, salt and pepper in screw- top jar; shake well.

# GRILLED VEGETABLE SALAD

1 medium red onion, cut into ¾- inch thick slices

1 medium eggplant, cut cross-wise into 1- inch thick slices

2 large red sweet peppers cut into ¾ - inch thick rings

1 medium zucchini, sliced lengthwise into ¼- inch slices

1 medium yellow squash, sliced lengthwise into ¼- inch slices

6 thin asparagus spears ¼ cup olive oil

Fresh ground pepper salt (optional)

6 cups torn mixed greens

¼ cup balsamic vinegar

¼ cup snipped fresh basil


Brush the prepared vegetables with olive oil and sprinkle each side with salt and pepper, if desired.

Lay vegetables perpendicular to wires on the rack of an uncovered grill directly over medium to medium–hot coals.

Grill onions, eggplant, and pepper rings for 8 to 10 minutes.

Grill zucchini, squash, and asparagus for 5 to 6 minutes or until crisp and tender, turn occasionally.

# MACARONI SALAD

½ cup uncooked macaroni

½ cup canned green peas, chilled

¼ lb. cheddar cheese, cubed

Salt and pepper to taste

1 hard cooked egg, sliced

¼ lb. ham cubed

½ cup celery, chopped

½ cup onion chopped

1 tbsp. parsley, minced

¼ cup green pepper, chopped

1/3 cup salad dressing

Cook macaroni according to package directions.
Toss all of these ingredients together, except egg.
Then Chill.
Garnish with egg slices.

# Soups

# CAULIFLOWER SOUP

½ head cauliflower

1 cup chicken stock or bouillon

3 tablespoons all- purpose flour

1 cup whipping cream

1 ½ cups milk

Salt and white pepper to taste


Break cauliflower into small flowerets
Bring stock to a boil in a large saucepan
Add cauliflower; cook 5 to 8 minutes or until tender

# CRAB SOUP

2 cans of mushroom soup

2 cans cream of celery

2 cans of cream of corn

2 cans of shrimp soup

2 sticks of butter (you may add another stick if you would like)

2 quarts of half and half

6 cans of crab meat

1 and 1/2 bunch green onions chopped

1 and 1/2 tablespoon shrimp boil

4 teaspoons of sherry

Season salt to taste


Heat all of the above ingredients together the longer it cooks the better it taste so enjoy.

# MIMI'S MEATY SOUP

3 tablespoons vegetables oil

1 garlic clove, minced

1 onion, chopped

1 red-bell pepper, seeded, chopped

½ lb. pepperoni or other hot sausage, casing removed, sliced

2 tomatoes, peeled, seeded, chopped

1 zucchini, chopped

1 small eggplant, peeled, chopped

6 to 8 cups beef stock

1-1/2 cups diced cooked beef

1 tablespoon tomato paste

Freshly chopped herbs

Salt and pepper to taste

Heat the oil in a large stock pot.
Add garlic, onion red pepper and pepperoni;
Sauté 10 minutes.
Add tomatoes, zucchini and eggplant; Cook 5 minutes

# POTATO SOUP

5 medium size white potatoes

1 can cream of mushroom soup

1 quart milk scalded pieces of chicken or ham, optional

A pinch of red pepper

1 can peas

4 large carrots

1 stick margarine

2 heaping tablespoon chopped fresh parsley

Salt

½ cup milk

Peel and slice potatoes. Cover with water and put to boiling.
Peel and grate carrots, set aside.
Heat the peas slightly in a sauce pan through a sieve.
Discard the hulls, leaving only the puree. Set aside.
Measure ½ cup of water and add to the mushroom soup and heat
the two ingredients in a sauce pan until bubbly, stirring constantly.
Set aside.

# SHRIMP SOUP

1 tbsp. vegetable oil

1 tbsp. flour

2 onions, chopped

1 ½ quarts water

2 quarts peeled, fresh shrimp

2 tomatoes

Salt, black and red pepper


Brown flour and onions in vegetables oil add shrimp and tomatoes. Add water and cook on low heat for 1 ½ hours you could add fresh corn cut from the cob, if you would like this is optional.

# WHITE BEAN SOUP

¼ pound bacon, cut into ¼- inch pieces

1 cup chopped onion

1 carrot, chopped

½ cup chopped turnip

4 cups chicken stock or broth

2 cups canned white kidney beans with the juice.

½ cup barley

Salt and freshly ground pepper

In a three quart saucepan over medium heat, cook the bacon and onions until the bacon is lightly browned and onions are translucent, about four minutes.

Add remaining ingredients. Bring to boil.

Reduce heat and simmer, covered, stirring often for about 30 minutes or until barley is cooked.

Adjust consistency with more chicken stock or water if desired. Use salt and pepper to taste.

# MAIN COURSES

# ASPARAGUS SPEARS ROLLED IN HAM

18 canned asparagus spears

¾ cup salad oil

¼ teaspoon salt

¼ cup wine vinegar

Freshly ground black pepper to taste

½ teaspoon dried basil

9 slices of thin boiled or baked ham

Marinate asparagus in oil, vinegar, salt, pepper, and basil for 2 hours.

Drain thoroughly. Cut ham crosswise and wrap around asparagus spears securing with a wooden pick.

May be prepared ahead of time.

# BAKED BEANS

4 bacon slices

1 small onion, finely chopped

3 cans pork and beans

½ cup barbecue sauce

3 tablespoons brown sugar

2 tablespoons prepared mustard


Cook your bacon in skillet until crisp, remove bacon and drain on paper towels, reserving 2 tablespoons of the drippings in skillet. Crumble bacon, and set aside.

Sauté the onions in hot drippings in skillet until tender.

Stir together onions, beans and next add 3 cans of pork in beans, ½ cup barbecue sauce, and 3 lbs. brown sugar place into a 2- quart baking dish. Sprinkle with bacon bake at 350 degrees for 1 hour.

# BAKED CHICKEN

2 large chickens cut in serving pieces

1 cup chopped onion

1 cup chopped celery

1 cup chopped green pepper

1 can chicken gravy

¼ tsp. Tabasco

1 clove garlic

1 can mushrooms

1 cup red wine

1 cup olive oil

Rub chicken with salt and pepper.
Place in roasting pan with as little space between pieces as possible.
Cover with coarsely chopped onions, celery, pepper, and pour olive oil over all.
Bake covered in 375 degree oven for one hour.
Uncover and lift chicken to the top.

Add the wine and mushrooms.

Continue baking uncovered until brown. Stir in one can chicken gravy. Or make your own gravy. If you want thickened add 2 teaspoons of cornstarch and water and cook until thickened.

# BAKED OYSTERS

2 pints oyster drained

1 lemon, juiced

Salt and pepper to taste

1 tablespoon cream

4 chopped green onions

1 stick butter

Worcestershire and Tabasco sauce to taste

Unseasoned bread crumbs

¼ cup minced parsley

Drain oysters well and lay in a well buttered 8 inch pie pan or larger.
Make a sauce of butter, lemon juice, Worcestershire and Tabasco sauce.
Salt and pepper oysters well you can add a pinch of seasoned salt if you like.
Sprinkle with cream. Pour sauce over and sprinkle with bread crumbs.
Cover heavily with minced green onions and parsley.
Bake 30 or 35 minutes in a 350 degree oven.

# BAKED PORK CHOPS

3 tbsp. salad oil

1 ½ cup uncooked rice

6 large onion slices

6 tsp. chili sauce

½ tsp. Tabasco

6 lean pork chops

Salt to taste

6 lemon slices

3 cups tomato juice

In a Dutch oven, heat the oil, add the pork chops and brown them on both sides.

Remove the chops and drain off all but 4 tbsp. of fat.

Stir in the uncooked rice, coating all the grains with fat.

Arrange the chops on top and sprinkle seasoned salt.

Place a slice of onion, a slice of lemon and a spoonful of chili sauce on each chop.

Add the tomato juice and Tabasco cover and bake the chops until they are tender, about 1 hour in a 325 degree oven, then serve with a smile.

# BAKED RED FISH

1 large red fish seasoned with salt and pepper

1 can stew tomatoes

1 large onion chopped

4 pieces celery chopped

3 cloves garlic chopped

1 teaspoon catsup

2 bell peppers, chopped

2 bell peppers, chopped

Sauté onion in oil until clear, Combine remaining ingredients with 1 pint of water.

Cover and simmer for about 2 hours pour over red fish and bake at 350 for 45 minutes.

Serve over hot rice.

# BAKED STEAK

1 1/2lb. chuck or round steak, sliced ¼ inch thick

¼ cup green pepper chopped

1/3 cup white wine

1 pack brown gravy mix, 1and 1/2 teaspoon seasoned salt

1 medium onion chopped

1 teaspoon oregano

Preheat oven to 325 degrees. Arrange a layer of ½ of the meat in 8 ½ x 61/2 inch baking dish. Dust meat with 1 ½ teaspoon season salt, ½ the brown gravy mix.

Combine the onion, green pepper and oregano. Top with half this mixture. Repeat for second layer. Pour wine over meat and add seasonings.

Cover dish tightly with foil.

Place in oven and bake for 2 hours.

# BEEF WITH PEPPER

1 ½ tablespoon oil

1 clove garlic, crushed

1 lb. Beef cut in small thin pieces

Pepper to taste

2 tablespoon cornstarch

1 tablespoon water

1 cup green peppers, cut length wise

½ teaspoon fresh ginger, finely chopped

Heat pan; add oil and garlic. When garlic turns brown remove. (Do let garlic burn).

Add beef, and fry a few minutes.

Season with salt, pepper and add soup stock and continue to cook for a few seconds.

Add mixture of cornstarch, soy sauce and water.

Cook until sauce thickens, stirring slowly. Add peppers and ginger, heat thoroughly and serve hot.

Serve over cooked rice.

## BLACK-EYED PEAS

1 (16-ounce) package dried black-eyed peas

4 cups water

1 large onion, chopped

½ teaspoon of black pepper

¾ teaspoon of salt

1 pound ham steak, cut into ½ inch cubes or 2 ham hocks

4 jalapeno peppers this is (optional)

Bring first 6 ingredients, if desired jalapenos to a boil in a Dutch oven; cover reduce heat, and simmer 1 hour or until peas are tender. Cook for 1 hour.

# CHICKEN CACCIATORI

2 and1/2 to 3lbs. chicken, cut olive oil

1 large onion

1 bell pepper

1-15oz. tomato sauce

1 clove garlic

½ teaspoon red pepper

1 teaspoon salt or seasoned salt

1 teaspoon oregano

½ teaspoon black pepper

¼ teaspoon thyme

4oz. mushroom stems and pieces

Flour, salt and pepper the chicken pieces.
Brown the chicken pieces in olive oil (1/2in.) for about 20 minutes.
Add bell pepper and onion and sauté in oil.
Drain most of the oil from skillet. Pour tomato sauce, seasoning and mushrooms over chicken. Simmer until chicken is done this will take about 1 hour.

# CHICKEN COOKED IN FOIL

2 large chicken breasts

2 cups cooked rice

2 cups water

Salt and pepper

2 tbsp. paprika

2pkg. dried onion soup

1 can evaporated milk

Cook rice in water.
Place in double layer of foil.
Pour milk over rice. Sprinkle soup mix over it.
Place chicken on top.
Repeat with layer of rice, milk and soup.
Wrap tightly and bake at 350 for about 1 hour.

# COLLARD GREENS

4 bunches of greens

1 pack of ham hocks or your choice of meat

½ teaspoon pepper

½ teaspoon of accent

½ teaspoon seasoning salt, (your chose of seasoning salt)

1 or 2 tablespoon of vegetable oil

When preparing your collard greens first cut them and wash them, and make sure your collard greens are thoroughly clean.

In large pot place the meat that you will be using. You can use neck bones, ham hocks, smoke turkey or you own choice of meat.

Season the meat and let the meat boil in the pot first then add clean bunches of cut greens. Add 1/4 teaspoon of pepper, and ½ teaspoon of accent, and ½ teaspoon of Tony Creole seasoning and the vegetable oil stir well and let cook. Cook the greens for about an hour or until tender. Serve with a slice of hot cornbread or over rice if you like this is a great down home dish.

# COUNTRY FRIED STEAK

1 ½ to 2 lbs. round steak

Flour

Salt and pepper

½ cup water

1 onion

Oil


Wet the steak then dip in flour and brown in hot oil.
Sprinkle with salt and pepper; add ½ cup water.
Cover and simmer 3 minutes.
Top with 1 onion sliced, then for 1 hour you let simmer.

# CRAB CAKES WITH SAUCE

8 ounces lump crabmeat, drained

¼ cup soft breadcrumbs

2 tablespoon minced fresh parsley

1 tablespoon minced fresh basil

2 tablespoon Dijon mustard

1 tablespoon lemon juice

1 teaspoon minced fresh ginger

½ teaspoon salt

1 teaspoon dark sesame oil

½ coarsely ground pepper

1 large egg, lightly beaten

¼ cup butter

Stir together all of your ingredients and shape them into patties
Melt 2 tablespoons butter in a large nonstick skillet over medium heat.

Add crab cakes, and cook for 5 minutes on each side or until golden brown. Remove from skillet and keep warm.

# CREOLE CASSEROLE

2 med. Onions

3 pieces celery

2 bell pepper

1 teaspoon salt

½ cayenne peppers

1 tablespoon Worcestershire sauce

1 teaspoon hot sauce

1 bay leaf

Stock or water if you prefer

1lb. shrimp (peel and devein)

1lb. sausage (cut into slices)

1 ½ cup rice

1 chicken or hen (cut into parts)

In a pot add oil. Season the chicken and add to the pot, brown the chicken then add the sausage then add celery, bell pepper, onion, salt cayenne pepper.

Add rice and stir, after uncooked rice has cooked for 2 to 3 minutes.

# FLOUNDER

2 Large flounders

1 stick melted butter

Salt and pepper to taste

¾ tablespoon poultry season

1 large lemon

½ lemons sliced thin

1 ½ tablespoon parsley, minced

3 green onions diced tops and bottoms


Score flounder, lay lemon slices into slits
Melt butter. Add poultry seasoning, salt pepper, lemon juice,
Parsley, and diced onions.
Broil flounder in center of oven, basting with sauce,
Broil about 20 minutes. Fish should be flaky and moist when done.

# FRIED CHICKEN

2 frying size chickens cut into serving pieces

Flour

Oil for deep frying

2 eggs

2 tablespoon seasoning

1 can evaporated milk

Beat 2 eggs in a bowl until well mixed.
Add a little evaporated milk to the eggs and seasoning.
In another bowl, put enough flour to coat the chicken.
Season your chicken well with both salt and pepper.
Take a piece of the chicken, roll it into the flour and then dip it into the egg mixture and then back into the flour.
Repeat the process until all the pieces are coated.
In the meantime, heat the oil or shortening in a deep skillet or a heavy iron pot and fry until golden brown on all sides.
Drain on paper towels and serve.

# FRIED WONTONS

1 pound crabmeat

2 pound boned and skinned chicken breast

1 teaspoon salt

1 teaspoon pepper

1 teaspoon garlic powder

2 package wonton wrappers

2 eggs, lightly beaten, set aside in a bowl

Oil for deep frying

Diced crabmeat and chicken together, and add salt, garlic powder and pepper then wrap in wonton wrappers.

Place teaspoon of filling in center of each wonton wrapper.

Fold the wrappers to the center gently press edges together fold in half again lengthwise.

Pull the 2 bottom corners, press together to seal then

Deep fry the wontons at 350 degrees until they are brown and crispy.

Serve hot wontons are great with plum sauce.

# MACARONI AND CHEESE

½ lb. American cheese

1lb. sharp cheddar

¼ lb. Monterey jack

16oz. box elbow macaroni

4 cups evaporated can milk

1 stick of butter

1 teaspoon salt or to your taste

2 eggs

1 teaspoon black pepper (or to your taste)

In a large container shred all of the cheese.
Boil the macaroni for about 7 minutes.
Then arrange the cooked macaroni, cheese salt and pepper in a casserole dish.
Beat eggs and pour into your casserole dish, mix ingredient well.
Pour milk and melted butter into the dish and bake uncovered at 350 degrees for 1 hour or until golden brown.
You may add unsalted bread crumbs mixed with parmesan cheese on top of this dish or more of the shredded cheeses listed above. Enjoy.

# MARINADE ROUND STEAK

½ cup lemon juice

¼ cup salad oil

½ tsp. salt or season salt your choice

½ tsp. celery salt

2 ½ lbs. round steak

½ tsp. pepper

½ tsp. thyme

½ tsp. oregano

½ tsp. rosemary

2 cloves garlic, minced

Combine all ingredients except steak.
Marinate steak 4 to 5 hours, turning several times.
Cook on grill over hot coals to doneness you like.
Baste with marinade during broiling.

# MARINATED FLANK STEAK

2 cups chopped onions

1 cup salad oil or cooking oil

2/3 cup vinegar

4 crushed garlic cloves

2 teaspoon salt

½ teaspoon thyme

½ teaspoon marjoram

Pepper to taste

Meat tenderizer- use liberally

½ teaspoon soy sauce

Flank steak
Marinate at least 4 hours, Cook on grill. Slice thin and serve.

# MEAT LOAF

1 ½ lb. ground beef

1 cup medium cracker crumbs or seasoned bread crumbs

2 eggs, beaten

1 (8oz.) can seasoned tomato sauce

½ finely chopped onion

2 tbsp. chopped bell pepper

1 ½ tsp. salt

1 medium bay leaf, crushed fine

Dash of thyme

Dash of marjoram

Combine all ingredients, mix well.
Shape into loaf in shallow baking dish.
Garnish top with bell pepper rings and onion rings can also place bacon strips on top of meat loaf.
Bake for 1 hour or until done.

# MIMI'S SEAFOOD GUMBO

3 large spoons of lard if you do not want to use lard you may use oil.

3 spoons flour

1 large onion

2-3 cloves garlic

½ bell pepper

3 quart water

2 can crab meat

Several whole crabs

1 lb. peeled shrimp, oyster and liquid

½ cup parsley

3-4 chopped green onions

1 bottle of clam juice

Make a roux with the Lard and flour. You can use canola or vegetable oil instead of lard to make your roux.

Cook slowly, stirring until brown.

Cut up onion, garlic, bell pepper and add to roux.

Slowly add about 3 quarts of water, stirring while you pour.

Add salt or seasoned salt, pepper to taste, season well.

Then add 2 cans of fresh claw crabmeat and several cleaned whole crabs and cook about an hour.

Then add one or more pounds of raw peeled shrimp and liquid from a pint of oysters and clam juice cook until shrimp are done.

About 11 minutes before serving add the oyster then add chopped parsley and green onions about 30 minutes before serving.

Serve over rice.

# PAN-BROILED LAMB CHOPS

8 loin lamb chops, ¾ to 1 inch thick

1 large clove garlic halved

½ lemons juiced

2 tbsp. minced parsley

1 tablespoon oil

1 ½ tablespoon butter

Salt and pepper to taste

1 tablespoon worcestershire

½ stick butter

Trim fat from chops. heat oil and butter, Saute garlic.
Over medium high heat sear chops, and broil turning often until juices run pink, not red when pricked with a fork.
Remove, salt and pepper.
Salting after cooking helps retain juices.
Pour off cooking fat.
In hot skillet add lemon juice and scrape bottom of pan.
Return to the heat then add butter Worcestershire and fresh parsley.
Stir until blended. Serve with sautéed fresh mushrooms and tiny boiled and buttered glazed onions.

# PLUM SAUCE

1 cup of plum jam

1 teaspoon onion powder

1 tablespoon vinegar

¼ teaspoon allspice

¼ teaspoon ginger powder

1 dash of garlic salt

1/3 or ½ cup of water (measurements depend on the thickness of the jam)

Mix all the ingredients together well; then bring to a boil on low heat.
This plum sauce is made fast and easy.
Stir constantly for about 2 minutes.
Let sauce cool and enjoy with your wontons.

# RED BEANS AND RICE

1 ½ cup red beans, washed and drained

3 ½ cups of water

1 clove garlic, chopped

1 stalk celery, chopped

1 med. Onion, chopped

1 large bay leaf, crushed

2 tbsp. parsley, chopped


Cook beans in water, Season with salt and bacon drippings, ham or other seasoning meat.

Cook for 1 and 1/2 to 2 hours.

Add onions, garlic, celery, and bay leaf. Continue to cook over low heat for ½ to 1 hour.

If beans become too dry, add heated water or a can of broth.

2 tablespoon of sugar will improve the taste of the beans.

Serve over rice.

# ROAST

1 (5-6LB.) rump roast

1 teaspoon salt

1 teaspoon red pepper

1 teaspoon black pepper

1 bell pepper

2 cloves of garlic

¼ cup of parsley

1 large onion

2 teaspoon prepared mustard


Season the roast a day or so before cooking time if possible.
Chop onion, garlic, bell pepper and parsley
Season this mixture also with salt and pepper and prepared mustard
2 teaspoons.
Make deep gashes in roast and insert all of this seasoning inside.
Roast in a heavy black pot if you have one with about enough oil
to cover bottom of pot.
Cover and let simmer slowly, browning evenly, adding a little water
at a time when well-browned.

Cooking time will depend on whether you like your roast well done or medium rare.

Medium rare takes about 2 hours cooking time.

If you prefer it well done, for a tasty roast slit openings in roast and fill the slits with chopped onions, garlic, and green pepper; season meat with salt, pepper, garlic salt.

Bake covered with foil, at 350 degrees until tender and brown (20 minutes per pound).

Baste frequently because you don't want it to dry out.

## *SAUSAGE WITH TOMATO GRAVY*

1 lb. un-smoked pork sausage

1 can of tomato (diced or whole)

1 small onion chopped fine

1 teaspoon season salt

1 can of tomato paste

Slice and season the sausage, then brown sausage stirring so that sausage will not burn.
Drain off excess grease, add onion and tomatoes and tomato paste.
Cook over low heat for 20 minutes.
Serve hot over rice.

# SHRIMP AND PASTA

8 oz. linguine

1 lb. medium shrimp peeled and devein

1 teaspoon seasoning salt

2 tbsp. vegetable oil

¼ tsp. garlic powder

½ tsp. ground ginger

1 red bell pepper sliced into strips

8 oz. fresh snow peas pods or sugar snap peas

¾ cup water

2 tsp. cornstarch

¼ cup soy sauce

Cook linguine according to the package directions.
Sprinkle shrimp with 1 teaspoon of season salt.
Heat 1 tablespoon of oil in a 10 inch skillet over medium high heat.
Add shrimp, sprinkle with garlic powder and ginger.
Stir –fry 3 minutes or until shrimp are pink. Then set aside

Add remaining 1 tablespoon oil to skillet

Stir fry pepper strips and pea pods for 2 minutes or until vegetables are tender.

Combine water, cornstarch, soy sauce and pour into the skillet; cook 1-2 minutes or until thickened, stirring occasionally.

Return shrimp to skillet; heat through serve over linguine. This will make about four servings.

# SHRIMP CREOLE

1 large onion, chopped (about 1 cup)

2 tablespoon butter

1 clove garlic, minced

½ cup green pepper diced

½ cup celery, diced

1 ½ teaspoon salt

¼ teaspoon black pepper

¼ teaspoon red pepper

¼ teaspoon thyme

1/8 teaspoon rosemary

¼ bay leaves

1 cans tomatoes (1-lb.)

1 tablespoon cornstarch

1 can tomato sauce (15-oz)

1 lb. cooked large shrimp (boil 15 minutes in water)

Cook onion in butter until soft and transparent.
Add garlic and cook a minute longer.
Add green pepper, celery, salt, pepper, herbs and bay leaf.
Mix 2 tablespoon juice drained from tomatoes with cornstarch and set aside.
Add remaining tomatoes and tomato sauce to cooked vegetables;
Cover and simmer 10 minutes. Remove bay leaf, add cornstarch to the mixture and cook, stirring until sauce boils and thickens slightly.
Add shrimp and heat through.
Serve over rice.

Makes about six servings.

# STEAK IN WINE

1 lb. sirloin

½ stick butter

1 tsp. black pepper

1 tsp. salt

1 cup red wine, your choice

1 med. Onion

Cut your steak in bite size pieces.
Chop onion very fine, Sauté steak and onion until brown
Add wine, cook on high heat for 20 minutes and serve.

# VEAL SCALLOPINI

3 lb. boned veal cut in 1 ½ inch cubes

½ cup flour

½ teaspoon salt

1/8 teaspoon pepper

½ teaspoon salad oil

½ cup minced onion

¾ cup canned mushrooms

2 cans tomatoes

1 tablespoon sugar

1/8 teaspoon Worcestershire sauce

1 or 2 cans tomato sauce

½ teaspoon parsley

Coat meat with flour, brown in oil; add all other ingredients and bake approximately 1 ½ hours at 350 degrees.

# BREADS

# BANANA BREAD

½ cup shortening or buttered flavored Crisco

2 eggs

1 teaspoon lemon juice

1 teaspoon baking powder

1 cup nuts

1 cup sugar

1 cup mashed ripe bananas

2 cup flour

½ teaspoon salt

Cream shortening and sugar together. Add eggs, banana, and lemon juice.
Blend well. Sift together flour, baking powder and salt.
Add to mixture along with nuts. Bake in pan lined with 2 layers of waxed paper or parchment paper.
Bake 50 to 60 minutes at 375 degrees.

# BISCUITS

5 cup flour

1 teaspoon salt

1 teaspoon soda

1 cup shortening

3 tablespoon baking powder

3 tablespoon sugar

2 tablespoon warm water

2 cup buttermilk

1 yeast cake

Dissolve yeast in warm water.
Combine ingredients as you would for regular biscuits.
Store dough in tightly closed plastic bag or bowl in refrigerator.
Use as needed, do not let rise at anytime. Roll out and bake on greased pan in 450 degree oven for ten minutes.

# LEMON BREAD

½ cup butter

2 eggs

½ cup milk

1 teaspoon baking powder

Dash or pinch of salt

1 to 2 cups, nuts, chopped

1 cup sugar

Grated rind of 1 lemon

1 ½ cup of sifted flour

Cream butter and sugar until light, then beat eggs and rind.
Stir together flour, baking powder, and salt add 1/3 at a time,
alternating with the milk, to the egg and sugar mixture.
Fold in the nuts then pour into buttered loaf pan.
Bake at 350 degrees for 45 to 55 minutes.
While hot and still in the baking pan pour over it a mixture of ½
cup sugar and juice of one lemon.
Leave in pan for 10 minutes then turn out to cool leave glazed
side up.

# *QUICK BUTTERMILK ROLLS*

¾ cup very warm buttermilk

2 tablespoon sugar

1 tablespoon salt

1 pkg. dry yeast

6 tablespoon soft shortening

2- 2 ¼ cup of flour

Mix together the very warm buttermilk, sugar, and salt.
Sprinkle yeast into mixture and let dissolve.
Allow shortening to soften add flour and mix well.
Knead on lightly floured board.
Shape rolls and place on a greased baking pan, let rise until doubled,
then bake at 400 degrees for 14-20 minutes

# SOUR CREAM CORN BREAD

1 ½ cup self rising corn meal

½ cup oil

1 small can cream style corn

2 eggs

1 cup sour cream

2 tablespoon sugar

Mix well bakes at 350 degrees for forty five minutes

LINDA MARIE THOMAS

# ZUCCHINI BREAD

3 eggs

2 ¼ cup sugars

3 cups sifted flour

1 teaspoon salt

1 ¼ teaspoon baking powder

2 cup grated zucchini

1 cup oil

1 ½ teaspoon vanilla

1 tablespoon cinnamon

1 teaspoon soda

1 cup nuts

Beat eggs; continue beating and add oil, sugar, zucchini and flavoring.
Sift together all your dry ingredients, and then fold in the nuts.
Spoon into greased and floured loaf pans.
Bake at 350 degrees for one hour.

# CAKES & DESSERTS

# ALOHA COCONUT CAKE

1 cup sugar

1 cup butter

4 egg whites

2 cups cake flour

3 teaspoon baking powder

½ teaspoon salt

½ teaspoon almond or macadamia nuts

1 cup milk

1 teaspoon vanilla

Cream butter and sugar sift flour before measuring.
Sift with baking powder and salt.
Add alternately with milk to cream mixture, beat very well.
Fold in stiffly beaten egg whites.
Pour into three greased layer cake pans.
Then bake at 375 degrees about 20 minutes.

# FILLING

1 Fresh coconut grated

Milk from the coconut plus sweet milk to make 1 cup

½ stick butter

1 teaspoon vanilla

½ teaspoon almond extract

A dash or pinch of salt

1 cup sugar

1 teaspoon of flour

Combine coconut, sugar, flour, salt and milk.
Cook over low heat, stirring frequently, until liquid is reduced to about half.
Then remove from the heat. Add butter stir until melted. Cool add extracts and spread between layers of cake, allowing the juice to soak into your cake.

# APPLE CRISP

1 can of applesauce

2 cans of apple pie filling

1 teaspoon cinnamon

½ cup sugar

¼ stick of unsalted butter

# CRUMB TOPPING

1 and ½ cup of flour

½ cup margarine

1 cup sugar and a pinch of salt

Spread the apple pie filling into a pan then spread the applesauce over the top of that.

Then sprinkle cinnamon and sugar. Cut pieces of butter on the top of that.

Crumb topping melt the butter then add the flour, salt and the sugar. If crumb topping is to dry, add more butter to the recipe.

Bake the apple crisp for 20 minutes at 350 degrees until golden brown.

# APPLE DELIGHT

8 cups thinly sliced apples

Lemon juice

Soak apples in lemon juice so that they will not turn brown.
Then place apples in baking dish top with topping in a bowl 2 sticks.

## TOPPING

2 cups flour

2 sticks of butter

1 cup brown sugar

2 cups granola cereal or 2 cup oatmeal and use your hands to mix well.

Bake for 40 minutes in 350 degree oven.

# BANANA BAKE

6 medium bananas

1 ½ tablespoons butter

3 tablespoons brown sugar

Shredded coconut

1/3 cup fresh orange juice

Slice your bananas into halves then cut each banana lengthwise into halves.
Place on a greased 9 inch pan
Then drizzle the butter and orange juice over the bananas.
Sprinkle brown sugar and coconut on top
Bake at 375 degrees for 10 minutes.
Garnish with a sprig of mint and cherries.

# SWEET PECANS

2 med. egg whites

½ cup of packed brown sugar

2 dashes of vanilla extract

5 cups of pecans

Pre-heat your oven at 275 degrees then line cookie sheet with wax or parchment paper. Spray the wax paper with butter flavored cooking spray

Beat egg whites until they are stiff add brown sugar and vanilla then stir smooth.

Mix in pecans and stir until coated then place pecans on the cookie sheet and bake for about 15 minutes. Do not burn.

# CARROT CAKE

2 cups flour

2 teaspoon baking powder

1 ½ teaspoon soda

1 teaspoon salt

2 teaspoon salt

2 teaspoon cinnamon

4 eggs

1 ½ cup oil

2 cups sugar

2 cups grated carrots

1 small can crushed pineapple

½ cup chopped pecans

Stir together dry ingredients. Mix eggs, oil and sugar. Add dry ingredients a little at a time and beat well after each addition
Fold in carrots, pineapple and nuts.
Bake 350 degrees in 3-9 inch layers

# FROSTING

1 box sifted powdered sugar

1 stick butter

1 eight ounce package of cream cheese

1 ½ teaspoon vanilla

Cream well. Spread between layers and cover top and sides of cake.

# CHOCOLATE FROSTING

1 large egg

3 tablespoons butter or margarine

3 tablespoons fine sugar

3 tablespoons cocoa

1 teaspoon flavoring


In a mixing bowl, beat egg; all the other ingredients and beat until the consistency of whip cream.

This recipe is great on chocolate cake.

Decorate with walnuts or pecans.

If the icing should separate a little while in the mixing bowl, add an extra teaspoon of sugar.

Sometimes one is larger than another; therefore you need more sugar, or half sugar and half cocoa.

# COFFEE CAKE

8 ounces cream cheese

½ cup butter

1 ¼ cups

2 eggs

2 cups flour

1 teaspoon baking powder

¼ cup milk

1 teaspoon vanilla

¼ teaspoon salt

# TOPPING

2 tablespoon butter

1/3 cup brown sugar

1/3 cup flour

½ teaspoon cinnamon

In a bowl cream the butter and cream cheese.
Gradually add sugar, continuing to beat.
Add eggs, one at a time, beating after each addition.
Combine flour, baking powder, baking soda, and salt and add alternately with milk then add vanilla.
Spread in a greased cake pan
Combine topping ingredients until crumbly and sprinkle over cake top.
Bake in a 350 degree oven for about 35 to 40 minutes.

## CREAM CHEESE FROSTING

3 ounces cream cheese, softened

¼ cup butter or margarine

1 teaspoon vanilla extract

3 cups powdered sugar

Beat cream cheese and butter or margarine together.
Add powdered sugar and vanilla, beating until smooth and creamy.
If necessary add a few drops of milk or cream for good spreading consistency.

# DREAM CAKE

1 ¾ cups all purpose flour

1 teaspoon grated lemon peel

¾ teaspoon baking soda

½ teaspoon salt

½ cup butter, softened

1 cup sugar

4 eggs

½ cup sour cream

1 teaspoon lemon juice

¼ cup chopped nuts

Mix together flour, lemon peel, baking soda, and salt. Then set aside.

In a large bowl mix together, butter, and sugar, at medium speed until light and fluffy.

Then thoroughly blend in eggs, sour cream and lemon juice.

Add flour mixture, ½ cup at a time, beating on low speed just until blended.

Pour half of mixture into greased and floured 9x5x3 loaf pan.

Sprinkle with nuts. Top with remaining batter, with narrow spatula gently swirl through batter to marble.

Bake in preheated 325 degree oven until cake tester inserted near center comes out clean, 60 to 70 minutes.

Cool on wire rack 10minutes.

Remove from pan and cool completely.

Frost or dust with confectioner's sugar if desired. Makes one loaf.

# FROZEN STRAWBERRY

15 large marshmallows

2 tablespoon strawberry juice (can use 4 tablespoons)

3 oz. softened cream cheese

1 cup drained frozen strawberries

1 cup drained crushed pineapple

½ cup mayonnaise

Stir marshmallows and strawberry juice over low heat until melted. Remove from heat. Stir in cream cheese until smooth.
Stir in fruit and mayonnaise. Fold in whipped cream pour into 8 inch square pan. Freeze until firm.

# GERMAN CHOCOLATE POUND CAKE

2 cup sugar

4 eggs

1 cup shortening

2 teaspoon butter or butter flavored Crisco

2 teaspoon vanilla

3 cup sifted flour

1 cup buttermilk

½ cup sour cream

½ teaspoon soda

1 teaspoon salt

1 pkg. German sweet chocolate, softened


Cream the sugar and shortening. Add eggs, butter flavoring and mix well.
Sift flour, salt and soda.
Add to other mixture.
Add softened chocolate and blend.
Pour in a greased floured pan and bake at 325 for 1 ½ hours.

# ICE CREAM

4 large egg yoke

½ cup sugar

1 cup whipping cream

3 egg whites

½ cup fruit (what ever fruit that you want to flavor your ice cream)

In a bowl add 4 large egg yokes and ½ cup sugar and beat together until it is like ribbons, and fold in the flavor that you would like to add, then add 1 cup whipping cream.

Fold it in until smooth then add 3 stiffly beaten egg whites.

It might look a little rough but continue to folding, then freeze over night.

# KEY LIME PIE

Pre-baked 9- inch pie shell

Graham cracker crust

3 egg yolks

1 ¾ cups sweetened condensed milk

Juice of 3 limes

1 tablespoon sugar

# MERINGUE

3 large egg whites, at room temperature

½ teaspoon vanilla extract

¼ teaspoon cream of tartar

6 tablespoon super fine sugar

Prepare the pre-baked pie shell; cool completely.
Beat the egg yolks until thick and light.
Beat in the condensed milk, lime juice, and sugar.

Turn the filling into the pie shell.

Preheat the oven to 350. To prepare the meringue, beat the egg whites, vanilla, and cream of tartar until the mixture holds stiff and glossy.

All the sugar must be dissolved.

Spread the meringue over the filling, sealing it to the edge of the crust.

Bake 12 to 15 minutes or until golden brown.

Make sure cool before serving.

# LEMON FROSTING

3 tablespoon butter

3 cups confectioners sugar sifted

1 tablespoon grated orange rind

2 tablespoons lemon juice

1 tablespoon water

A pinch of salt


Cream butter; add orange rind and cream
Add about ¾ cup sugar gradually, blending after each addition.
Combine lemon juice and water; add to creamed mixture alternately
with remaining sugar until right consistency to spread.
Add the salt and beat until smooth.

# MISSISSIPPI MUD CAKE

1 ½ cup flour

2 cups sugar

½ cup cocoa

4 eggs

1 cup oil

3 tsp. vanilla

1/4 teaspoon salt

# CAKE ICING

1 box powered sugar

1 teaspoon vanilla

1 stick oleo, melted

1 cup walnuts

1/2 cup cocoa

1/2 cup evaporated milk

In a bowl mix eggs, oil, sugar, vanilla then slowly add flour and salt. Mix well

Pour into a greased and floured pan. Bake for 35 to 40 minutes at 350. Let your cake cool on rack then when cool frost it with chocolate icing.

# ORANGE CAKE

1 cup shortening

2 cups sugar

4 eggs separated

2 tablespoon orange rind

1 cup nuts

1 teaspoon soda

1 1/3 cups buttermilk

4 cups flour

1 package dates

Cream the butter and sugar.
Add egg yolks and beat.
Add buttermilk and flour alternately, saving ½ of the flour to dredge dates and nuts.
Add them with orange rind.
Beat egg whites until very stiff.
Fold into cake mixture. Bake in tube pan about 1 to ½ hours in 300 degree oven.
Remove from oven and while hot, pour sauce over.

# SAUCE

3 cups sugar

2 tablespoons orange rind

1 ½ cups orange juice

1 teaspoon lemon juice


Heat just long enough to melt sugar. Do not boil.
Pour over cake immediately. When cool pick up cake, which will
be resting on the tube section.

# PEACH COBBLER

2 cup fresh sliced peaches

1 cup sugar

Let this stand while mixing batter.
Melt ¼ lb. butter

# BATTER

1 cup sugar

¼ teaspoon salt

1 teaspoon baking powder

¾ cup flour

¾ cup milk

Mix the dry ingredients well then beat in the milk until there are no lumps.
Pour batter into the melted butter, and do not stir.
Spoon the sliced peaches over the top of the batter do not stir.
Bake 45 minutes in a 350 degree oven or until the top is golden brown.
Serve with fresh whipped cream.

# PECAN CANDY

1 ½ cup brown sugar

4 cups white sugar

½ lb. butter

2 cans evaporated milk

½ lb. butter

5 cups pecan chopped or you may leave whole

A pinch of salt

1 teaspoon vanilla

Place 2 can milk, ½ lb. butter, 4 cups white sugar 1 cup light brown sugar and a pinch of salt into a large heavy pan. Bring to a boil and cook to slowly stirring constantly.

This candy is difficult to make,

Remove from heat and add the remaining ½ lb. of butter beating constantly.

When you see that the candy is beginning to thicken, add the Pecans and vanilla.

When thick, drop quickly by teaspoon on a buttered surface or foil.

Leave 2 to 3 inches between each candy for each one will flatten. This candy is to be stirred constantly while being cooked and also as you remove it from the stove.

# PECAN NO-COOK ICE CREAM

½ cup light brown sugar

¼ cup sugar

3 cups half and half

1 ¼ cup broken pecan pieces

Combine sugars and half and half and blend or mix until the sugars are dissolved. Stir in the pecan pieces and refrigerate until chilled, about one hour.

Pour the mixture into an ice cream maker and freeze according to the manufacturer's direction until moderately set.

Continue freezing until the ice cream is firm. Serve immediately or pack the ice cream into an airtight container, cover tightly with plastic wrap and freeze up to three days.

This recipe makes about one quart.

# PINEAPPLE CAKE

2 cups sifted all- purpose flour

2 teaspoon soda

1 teaspoon salt

1 cup cooking oil

2 cups sugar

3 eggs

1 large can crushed pineapple with sugar added

1 cup pecans or walnuts chopped (optional)

Mix dry ingredients then add oil; eggs.
Stir in pineapple and mix well.
Add nuts and bake in a 9x12 inch pan at 350 degrees for 45 minutes.

# *ICING*

1 stick butter

1 box powdered sugar

1 eight ounce cream cheese

2 teaspoon vanilla

Cream all ingredients together and pour over cake while it is warm.

# PINEAPPLE PIE

1 can (20 ounces) crushed pineapple in syrup

1 package (3.5 ounces) instant lemon pudding and pie filling mix

1 cup milk

1 carton (4 ounces) frozen whipped topping, thawed

2 tablespoons lemon juice

1 teaspoon lemon zest

1 eight or ten inch graham cracker pie crust


Drain pineapple well. Then combine pudding mix and milk in a bowl.

Beat 2 to 3 minutes until very thick then fold in whipped topping and pineapple, lemon juice, and lemon zest.

Pour into pie crust. Cover and refrigerate to chill for 4 hours or overnight.

Garnish as desired.

# PINEAPPLE UPSIDE DOWN CAKE

¼ cup butter

¾ cup brown sugar

Canned pineapple

Walnuts

Maraschino cherries

## CAKE

¼ cup shortening

½ cup sugar

1 egg

1 cup milk

½ teaspoon vanilla

Melt butter in a 2 – inch high round pan.

Cover with brown sugar evenly.

Arrange pineapple slices in a pattern over the sugar, placing walnuts where desired to form a design.

Cream the shortening and sugar. Add eggs and beat.

Add flour alternately with milk, beating after each addition.

Add vanilla, than pour into pan over fruit.

Bake in a 350 oven for 40 to 50 minutes.

# SOUR CREAM TOPPING

8oz. sour cream

1 teaspoon vanilla

1 teaspoon maple syrup


In a bowl, add sour cream, vanilla and the maple syrup then pour over strawberries.

# STRAWBERRY DELIGHT

1 banana

½ plain yogurt

1 tablespoon Rum

1 ½ tablespoon sugar, or to taste

Strawberries

In a blender put a banana then ½ plain add a little bit of Rum blend then add some sugar to the strawberries that you have sitting in the bowl.

Take some of those strawberries, Place in a glass then pour some of the yogurt mixture on top of them, add some more strawberries then more, yogurt and continue the layering process until the glass is full.

# SWEET POTATO PIE

1 ½ cups mashed sweet potato

3 tablespoon flour

2/3 cup evaporated milk

1 teaspoon vanilla

1 stick melted butter

1 ½ cups sugar

2 eggs

1 teaspoon lemon or vanilla extract

Combine all ingredients and pour into a 9 inch unbaked pie shell. Bake at 375 degrees. Test with knife or tooth pick after 45 minutes.

# TASTY POUND CAKE

8 eggs separated

6 tablespoons sugar

1 lb. butter

1 ¾ cups sugar

3 ½ cups flour

½ cup light cream

1 tablespoon vanilla

Separate eggs and beat white stiff with 6 tablespoons sugar.
Place in refrigerator. Cream the butter and sugar, and egg yolks.
Alternate flour and cream, then add vanilla.
Fold in stiffly beaten egg whites.
Bake in a tube cake pan at 325 degrees oven for 1 ½ hours.

# TOASTED ALMOND BUTTER CAKE

½ cup butter or margarine, softened

½ cup shortening

2 cups sugar

5 large eggs, separated

2 ¼ cups all purpose flour

1 ¼ teaspoon baking soda

1 cup plus 2 tablespoons buttermilk

1 teaspoon almond extract

½ teaspoon vanilla extract

½ teaspoon butter flavoring

1 cup slivered almonds, toasted and chopped

Cream cheese frosting

½ cup slivered almonds, toasted

Beat butter and shortening at medium speed with an electric mixer until creamy.

# VANILLA FROSTING

4 tablespoons butter

2 cups confectioners' sugar sifted

1 teaspoon vanilla

3 tablespoon milk

A pinch of salt


Cream butter; and 1/3 cup sugar gradually, blending after each addition.

Add remaining sugar alternately with milk, beating after each addition until right consistency to spread. Add vanilla and salt.

# WHITE FROSTING

1 cup sugar

1/8 teaspoon salt

1/8 teaspoon cream of tarter

¼ cup cold water

2 eggs whites

1 ½ teaspoon vanilla extract


Mix the first 5 ingredients in top of double boiler.
Beat at low speed with an electric mixer 30 seconds.
Place over boiling water; beat at high speed 7 minutes or until
stiff peaks form. Remove from heat.
Add vanilla; beat 2 minutes or until thick enough to spread.

# DIPS

# CHEESY ONION DIP

1 Package of dry onion soup mix

2 cups of sour cream

1/2 teaspoon of onion powder

¾ cup of shredded sharp or mild cheddar cheese

2 dashes of Louisiana hot sauce.

In bowl mix soup mix, sour cream and all other ingredients together. Place in a tightly sealed container and refrigerate once chilled you can serve dip with vegetables or your favorite chips.

# CRAB COCKTAIL

1 cup frozen crab meat thawed

1 cup mayonnaise

2 tbsp. catsup

1 tbsp. lemon juice

1-1lb. can grapefruit section, chilled and drained

Add a few drops of Tabasco sauce, flake crab meat; sprinkle with lemon juice.
Alternate grapefruit sections and crab meat in salad bowls.
Combine remaining ingredients; pour over the grapefruit and crab meat.

# FRUIT DIP

1 oz. jar of marshmallow

8 oz. package of cream cheese

1 tablespoon lemon juice or lime juice


Blend all ingredients together well.
Use any fruit that you like to dip. I use Pineapples and Strawberries.

# GUACAMOLE

2 ripe avocados

The juice of 1 lemon

1 garlic clove

1 teaspoon salt

1 teaspoon grated onion

Mash avocados and mix with all the other ingredients, remove garlic clove before serving.

# HOT CRAB DIP

1 eight ounce package cream cheese

2 cans crab meat

1 lb. Velveeta cheese

2 tablespoon grated onion

Dash of Worcestershire sauce

1 tomato, chopped

Dash of seasoned salt


Blend all of the above ingredients into a baking dish.
Bake at 350 degrees for 20 minutes then serve with crackers.

# JAMAICAN JERK RUB

1/3 cup freeze dried chives

1 table spoon fine grain sea salt

1 tablespoon onion powder

1 tablespoon dried onion flakes

1 tablespoon garlic powder

1 tablespoon ground ginger

1 tablespoon dried thyme

1 tablespoon light brown sugar

1 tablespoon ground red pepper

2 teaspoon ground allspice

2 teaspoons coarsely ground black pepper

2 teaspoon ground coriander

1 teaspoon ground cinnamon

½ teaspoon ground nutmeg

½ teaspoon ground cloves

Process all ingredients in a blender until ground and well blended.

If you have or make extra amounts of rub store it in an air tight container for use on all cuts of chicken and pork.

Tip: Hickory chips give Jamaican Jerk Chicken an extra smoky flavor.

# *SHRIMP DIP*

8 ounce cream cheese

¼ teaspoon onion

Dash of Worcestershire

Dash of paprika

1/3 cup of sour cream

2 teaspoon freshly squeezed lemon juice

1 ½ cup chopped cooked shrimp

A dash of garlic salt

In a bowl soften cheese and blend in sour cream and seasonings.
Stir in shrimp and add paprika

# TARTAR SAUCE

2 cups mayonnaise

2 tablespoons white wine vinegar

3 scallions minced

3 sweet gherkins minced

¼ cup

2 tablespoon capers drained

In a large bowl combine all ingredients cover and refrigerate until cold this sauce can be kept in the refrigerator for up to one week if you seal it properly in a container.

# VEGETABLE DIP #1

2/3 cup mayonnaise

2/3 cup sour cream

1 tablespoon dried onions

1 tablespoon dried parsley

1 teaspoon seasoned salt

1 teaspoon accent

1 teaspoon dill

Mix all of the above ingredients and serve with fresh vegetables.

# VEGETABLE DIP #2

1 ½ cup sour cream

2 ½ cup mayonnaises

1 cup finely chopped onion

1 cup finely chopped green pepper

½ finely chopped pimento

½ teaspoon pepper

¼ teaspoon garlic powder

¼ teaspoon Tabasco or hot sauce

Combine all ingredients in large bowl and stir to blend well. Cover bowl and chill at least one hour or overnight.

Breinigsville, PA USA
07 September 2009
223658BV00001B/101/A